Stories of Courage

Clare Gray

Level 3

Series Editors: Andy Hopkins and Jocelyn Potter

Pearson Education Limited
Edinburgh Gate, Harlow,
Essex CM20 2JE, England
and Associated Companies throughout the world.

ISBN: 9781447967606
First edition published 2004
This edition published 2007

3 5 7 9 10 8 6 4 2

Text copyright © Clare Swain 2004
Illustrations by Enrique Flores, maps on page 9 by Witmor

Set in 11/13pt A. Garamond
Printed in China
SWTC/02

Produced for the Publishers by AC Estudio Editorial S.L.

Published by Pearson Education Ltd

Acknowledgements

We are grateful to the following for permission to reproduce photographs:
Alamy Images: page 43 (c) (Dynamic Graphic Group), (d) (Nick Onken/OnRequest Images Inc.);
John Birdsall: page 43 (a); **Steve Bloom Images:** page 19; **Ecoscene:** page 21; **Empics:** page iv (c) and page
23 and page 40 (AP Photo/AJB), page iv and page 26 (AP Photo), page 28 and page 40 (AP Photo), page 35
(AP/Damian Dovarganes), page 38 (AP/Junji Kurokawa), page 39 (AP/Itsuo Inouye); **Eyevine:** page 29,
page 30 and page 31; **Getty Images:** page iv and page 3, page 2 (AFP), page 4, page 15 and page 40, 16 and
page 18 (a) and (b) (Hulton Archive), page 27 (Time Life Pictures), page 37 (Hulton Archive), page 44 (Stone);
National Portrait Gallery: page 18 (c) (Mark Gerson 1921); **PunchStock Royalty Free Images:** page 43 (b)
(ImageSource); **Rex Features:** page 33; **TopFoto:** page 20 (ImageWorks)
Picture research by Kath Kollberg / Karen Jones

For a complete list of the titles available in the Pearson English Active Readers series, visit www.pearsonenglishactivereaders.com.
Alternatively, write to your local Pearson Education office or to
Pearson English Readers Marketing Department, Pearson Education, Edinburgh Gate, Harlow, Essex CM20 2JE, England.

Contents

1.1 What's the book about?

1 This book is about brave people. Who do you know who is/was very brave? Make notes on two people in the box. Then tell another student about them.

Name	Brave Act(s)
1	
2	

2 Match each of the pictures (A–D) with a sentence below.

1 ☐ This person is still fighting for Burma's freedom today.
2 ☐ This young American lost an arm in a terrible accident.
3 ☐ This famous runner won gold medals for Cuba.
4 ☐ This person wanted to protect the trees around the Amazon from big business.

1.2 What happens first?

Look at the title of Story 1, the words below it, and the pictures in the story. Are these sentences about Ana Quirot true (✓) or not (✗)? What do you think?

1 ☐ Ana will become the fastest woman in Cuba.
2 ☐ Ana will win an Olympic gold medal.
3 ☐ Ana will have an accident.
4 ☐ Ana will go to the hospital.
5 ☐ Ana will lose a leg.

Running for her Life

Ana woke up. Fidel Castro was by her bedside. "I will run again,"
she told him. Then her eyes closed.

Ana Fidelia Quirot was born in a small town in the east of Cuba. She was a happy child and from an early age she loved running. Sports were important to her family and they were important to Cuba, too. The Cuban government wanted to produce the best doctors, the smartest teachers, and the strongest sports players in the world. There were special government schools for intelligent young scientists and for children who were good at sports.

By the time she was ten years old Ana could run very fast. Soon she was winning races—often without shoes! She wanted someone from a government sports school to see her. Ana knew that only Cuba's best students were chosen. So she practiced hard every day. At last she heard the news that she was waiting for. At thirteen she had a place at a government sports school. "If I work hard," she thought, "I can be the fastest girl in Cuba."

The other children at Ana's new school were tall and strong. But Ana's body was changing. She stopped growing taller and started growing fatter. She felt heavier too, so she practiced less often. Ana's future did not seem bright and exciting to her now.

But when Ana's school asked her to leave, she thought very carefully. She realized that she loved her school and her life there. It was her dream and she did not want to lose it. Luckily, Blas Beato, one of Cuba's most famous running teachers, knew about Ana. She was heavy, but she was strong and fast. Beato could see that. "Try the 400-meter race," he said. "I think you can be the best."

It was not easy, but with Beato's help, Ana quickly became thinner. She pushed her body hard, and began winning races at school again. Soon she was the fastest girl in Cuba at 400 and 800 meters. Her mind became stronger, too. She learned to fight against pain and to believe in her dreams.

Ana finished school and practiced harder and longer every day. In 1987 she won two gold **medal**s at the Pan American Games* in Indianapolis, in the US, and in 1989 she won *all* of her 800-meter races. Ana was very proud to run for her country. Now her name was famous around the world.

---

* Pan American (Pan Am) Games: the biggest and most important sports games for North, South, and Central American countries. They happen every four years.

medal /'medl/ (n) a flat piece of metal, used as a prize

Four years after her double gold medal success in Indianapolis, Ana was ready to run again in the Pan Am Games. These races were very important to Ana because the Pan Am Games were coming to Cuba. She was Cuba's most famous runner—and her country was watching her.

Ana's races were fast and exciting. She ran faster than the other runners in the 400- and 800-meter races—two more gold medals! Ana looked up at the crowd. Thousands of happy Cubans were calling her name and smiling. Ana turned and walked slowly toward her country's president, Fidel Castro. Then she took one of her medals and placed it around Castro's neck. It was her way of saying "thank you" to Cuba, her country. She felt proud of the past and excited about the future. But early the next year, Ana's dreams were destroyed before they started.

◆

On January 23, 1993, Ana was washing some clothes. She was washing in the Cuban way, in a large bowl on top of a stove. She carefully added a little **alcohol** to the washing to make the clothes fresh and bright. But some alcohol fell onto the stove. In seconds, fire covered Ana's body. She moved away from the stove and tried to pull her sweater off, but the fire quickly reached her skin. Ana's body burned with heat and pain. She fell heavily to the floor.

alcohol /ˈælkəˌhɔl, -ˌhɑl/ (n) the part of drinks like beer that makes people drunk; strong *alcohol* is also used for cleaning.

The doctors at Havana's Hermanos Ameijeiras Hospital worked hard to save their famous patient. People all over Cuba listened carefully to the radio news. Ana's friends and family hurried to her bedside. Bad burns covered 38% of Ana's body and she was close to death.

A few days later, Ana woke up. Fidel Castro was by her bedside. "I will run again," she told him. Then her eyes closed.

Ana spent five long months in the hospital. Slowly she became stronger. First, she began walking around her room. Sometimes she cried with pain and sadness. "You must rest," her friends told her. But Ana did not listen. Every day she walked a little farther. She refused to stop fighting.

Only a month after her accident, Ana began walking around inside the hospital. After two months she was running up and down the hospital stairs—fifteen floors! Next, she asked for an exercise bike in her hospital room. The

doctors could not believe their eyes. Ana Quirot was winning again—winning against pain. "If I don't run again," she said, "I will die."

The skin on Ana's hands, arms, and stomach was very badly burned. She could not move the top part of her body freely. It was very difficult for her to walk without pain. It was almost impossible to run well. But Cuba's best doctors carefully repaired her body. It was hard, slow work.

Ana went home and started running outside, but the sun's heat was too strong for her. Her skin was weak and it burned very easily. She could only practice very early in the morning and late at night. This problem did not stop her.

Ana worked hard that year. She wanted to run for her country again. But she was in her thirties now—too old for an international runner, people said. Ana did not agree. In 1993, the same year as her terrible accident, she ran at the Central American and Caribbean Games in Puerto Rico. Ana was not able to move her arms or head easily at this time, but she surprised everyone. She ran well, and won a silver medal in the 800-meter race. The crowd loved it. "She won the silver medal in the race," Castro said, "but she won a great gold medal for **courage**."

By 1995 Ana was running internationally. That summer she won the gold medal for 800 meters in the World Games in Stockholm, Sweden. She was one of the fastest women in the world—again! "In my most difficult times," she said, "I didn't think that I could come back so strongly."

Ana raced many strong, young runners in 1996. At thirty-three years old she was often the oldest woman in her race. But now it was almost time to rest her body and mind. There was one more important race to run. "If I can run in the Olympic Games again, I will be happy," she said.

The 1996 Olympic Games were in Atlanta, US. Some of the fastest women of all time were there: Maria Mutola of Mozambique, the American Meredith Rainey, and Svetlana Masterkova of Russia. The early races were very hard for Ana, but she ran fast and well. Now, in the finals, she could race against the world's best runners at the Olympics one more time. In her mind, this was her last big race. The other women were younger and stronger. Ana was happy to be with them. "I will run as fast as possible," she thought. It was a difficult race, but Ana won the silver medal—she was less than a second behind Masterkova!

Ana walked off the airplane at Havana into the warm Cuban air. It was good to be home. She was Cuba's most famous, and favorite, runner. "Running, and my country, saved my life," she explained. "When I started running again, that gave me life." Ana Quirot's fight against pain and illness is an example of courage for us all.

courage /ˈkɔːɪdʒ, ˈkʌr-/ (n) fearlessness at a difficult or dangerous time

2.1 Were you right?

Look back at your answers to Activity 1.2 on page iv. Then add the correct information below.

When?	What happened?
Age 13	
1987	
	She had a terrible accident. She was badly burned.
	She won gold for the 800 meters in Stockholm.
1996	

2.2 What more did you learn?

How did Ana solve her problems? Match each problem (1–5) with its answer (A–E).

1 [B] Ana's school asked her to leave, so …
2 [ ] Ana was badly burned in the accident, so …
3 [ ] After her accident, Ana wanted to run again, so …
4 [ ] Ana wanted to exercise in her hospital room, so …
5 [ ] Ana's skin burned easily in the Cuban sun, so …

A   she asked for an exercise bike.
B   she became thinner.
C   she practiced in the early morning and late at night.
D   she started walking around her hospital room.
E   she was looked after by Cuba's best doctors.

2.3 Language in use

1 **Look at the sentence in the box. Then answer these questions.**

> Sometimes she cried with **pain** and **sadness.**

   a How did Ana's body feel? ....painful........

   b How did Ana feel? ....

2 **Now complete the second sentence in each pair so it has a similar meaning to the first.**

   a She laughed happily.

      She laughed with ....happiness.............. .

   b She dreamed about winning.

      Winning was her ....

   c She felt very excited.

      She felt great ....

   d She was careless with the alcohol.

      She didn't take .... with the alcohol.

   e Her work on the exercise bike was successful.

      Her work on the exercise bike was a ....

   f The sun was too hot for her skin.

      The sun's .... was too strong for her skin.

2.4 What's next?

Look at the pictures in Story 2. The story is about a brave African man called Matthew. Discuss these questions and make notes below.

1 What kind of dangers will Matthew face, do you think?

2 How will he escape from these dangers?

Notes

The River to Freedom

*Suddenly, the crocodile turned and swam away. It was
not Matthew's first lucky escape—or his last.*

The big African sun was low in the sky and the Nile River moved slowly and quietly through the wide land. Matthew's clothes felt cold against his skin in the water. He **float**ed silently, listening carefully for soldiers' voices. "They will kill me if they find me," he thought. He stayed carefully by the long grass at the side of the river.

Matthew's body hurt and he was hungry and very weak. He wanted to swim quickly to safer water, but he did not move. Soldiers can easily hear the sound of a man swimming on a quiet evening. Matthew looked slowly around the dark river—straight into the narrow, yellow eyes of a **crocodile**!

float /fləʊt/ (v) to stay on or near the top of the water like a ship
crocodile /ˈkrɑkəˌdaɪl/ (n) a large, dangerous water animal; it has a long tail and a long mouth with lots of teeth

The large, dangerous animal began swimming quickly toward him. What could he do? "I'm a dead man!" he thought. As the animal came closer, Matthew looked deep into its cold eyes. He prepared for a painful death.

Suddenly, the crocodile turned and swam away. It was not Matthew's first lucky escape—or his last.

◆

Six months earlier, Matthew was enjoying a quiet evening with his father. They were sitting outside their home in the south of Sudan, talking happily. Suddenly, soldiers arrived in the quiet streets near them. "We didn't say anything," he remembers. "We waited for a question ... but there was no question ... They came and shot my father. I couldn't believe that my father was shot."

Matthew wanted to destroy his father's murderers immediately. Moving quickly toward the soldiers, he tried to take a gun. But he was one man against many. He was caught and taken to an **army** prison. He was one more prisoner in Sudan's long war.

Matthew's room in prison was too small for a bed. It was even too low to stand up in. It was a painful and difficult life. But Matthew stayed in this dark box for six months. Every day the soldiers hit the prisoners. Matthew's body was weak and broken, but his mind and heart were still strong.

One day the prison guards decided to move some of the prisoners. Did they want to kill them? Or was Matthew's luck changing at last? As he walked slowly and painfully in the bright sun, Matthew noticed something like an ugly, gray stream. It was cut straight and deep into the earth. Dirty water ran through it from the prison buildings, through the yard, and under the prison wall.

army /ˈɑrmi/ (n) a country's soldiers; *armies* fight on land

"I asked a guard where the water went," Matthew remembers. It ran into the Nile. Matthew's hope grew stronger. But the guard knew what Matthew was thinking. "Don't try to go there," he said. "You're already a dead man." The guard described the **power**ful electricity lines that crossed the water near the prison walls. "If you touch those lines," he continued, "you will die!"

Matthew's hope was almost destroyed. His life in prison was terrible, his father was dead, and his body was weak. Then he looked at the other broken men around him. He knew that he had to try.

At around 5:30 P.M. the smell of food floated from the prison kitchen in the warm evening air. As the line of prisoners walked across the yard for their small, tasteless meals, Matthew stayed near the back. Then he suddenly turned away from the other prisoners and jumped quickly into the gray water.

Matthew's eyes closed, and now he remembers nothing about that time. His weak body was carried by the water under the electricity lines, and from one type of danger to another.

power /ˈpaʊə/ (n) a strong position over other people; they must do what you say

When he woke up at the side of the river, his head and leg hurt badly. He was lucky to be alive. But he was not safe yet. He had to leave Sudan to save his life. For days he floated without sleep or food. But as Matthew's courage carried him north, it also carried him away from his painful past.

It is difficult to leave your country, your friends, and your family. But Matthew had a plan. He knew some people in Port Sudan, on Sudan's east coast. "I have to find my friends before the soldiers find *me*," Matthew realized. There was no time to rest.

He left the river, turned east, and started walking. For three and a half months he traveled overland, keeping away from people and towns. Every day he felt hungry and lonely. But he bravely fought his fears and feelings.

Tired and weak, Matthew arrived in busy Port Sudan. He wanted to stay with his friends in the city. But that was dangerous for all of them. He had to leave. He found a ship and said goodbye to his friends and his country. It was a brave step toward an unknown future. But Matthew was a strong man. He knew how to find the courage for each new problem. He was full of hope for the future.

◆

Today Matthew (not his real name) lives happily in Sofia, Bulgaria. His new European friends know him as a big, tall man. But his true **strength** is much greater than the eye can see.

strength /strɛŋθ, strɛnθ/ (n) the opposite of weakness

3.1 Were you right?

Look back at Activity 2.4. Then put these sentences in the right order, 1–8.

- ☐ Matthew left Sudan on a ship.
- ☐ Matthew lived in a small, dark prison room for six months.
- ☐ Matthew walked through Sudan for three and a half months.
- 1 Soldiers killed Matthew's father.
- ☐ Matthew jumped into the gray water in the prison.
- ☐ Matthew had a lucky escape from a crocodile.
- ☐ Water carried Matthew's body under the electricity lines.
- ☐ The soldiers took Matthew to prison.

3.2 What more did you learn?

Look at these pictures. How are these things important in Story 2? Write a sentence about each one.

A ....

B ....

C ....

D ....

3.3 Language in use

Look at the sentences in the box. Then complete the sentences below with the correct verb forms. Use these verbs:

> Matthew **was enjoying** a quiet evening with his father. Suddenly, soldiers **arrived**.

stay	float	lose	go	notice	catch	see
	decide	move	find	try	jump	

1 Matthew .... was trying .... to take a soldier's gun when the soldiers .... him.

2 Matthew .... hope in prison when he .... to escape.

3 The guards .... the prisoners. Suddenly, Matthew .... the stream.

4 When Matthew suddenly .... into the stream, the other prisoners .... to the kitchen for food.

5 Matthew .... a crocodile when he .... in the river.

6 He .... in Port Sudan when he .... a ship for Bulgaria

3.4 What's next?

Story 3 is about Odette Sansom—a spy in World War 2. What do spies do in wartime? Make notes on five different jobs.

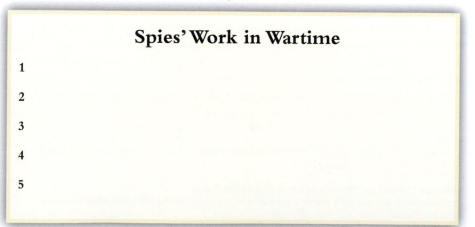

Spies' Work in Wartime

1

2

3

4

5

The Housewife Spy

"We want you to go to France as a spy," the man said calmly. Odette could not believe her ears. A spy? Her? Was this man crazy?

Odette was born in Amiens, in the north of France, in 1912. During World War I her mother helped the fight against Germany by offering rooms in her home to British soldiers. Little Odette loved playing with the soldiers. They spoke strangely, but they were friendly and interesting. She loved their stories about England. When Odette later married an Englishman, her mother was not surprised! After a short time in France, Odette and her husband moved to England in 1931.

In 1939 German soldiers attacked Poland, and World War II began. One year later, Germans moved into France and started a new government there. Odette's heart was broken. She remembered the proud people of Amiens in World War I. They fought hard for France's **freedom**, but now it was lost. Odette knew that she wanted to help. But she was only a **housewife**. What could she do?

In the early 1940s more and more countries joined the war. Around the world, people were fighting and dying. Odette listened to the radio news sadly, and then her heart stopped...The British government wanted pictures of French beaches! Her old vacation photos! At last she could really help.

When the British Secret Service* saw Odette's photos, they immediately became interested in this young Frenchwoman. She knew a lot about the north of France. Maybe she had some more useful information. Or maybe she could help in another way. Was she smart? Was she brave? Did she want to help Britain and France? They decided to invite Odette to their offices in London. Soon Odette was traveling toward a future that she could not imagine in her wildest dreams.

"We want you to go to France as a spy," the man said calmly. Odette could not believe her ears. A spy? Her? Was this man crazy?

"I'm only a housewife," she replied quietly. "I have three young daughters and a loving husband. They need me. I'm sorry."

But as Odette listened to her own voice, she knew. She knew that her country needed her more. The room was quiet. The calm man sat silently

---

* British Secret Service: the part of the British government that tries to find secret information. This is most important during wars.

freedom /ˈfriːdəm/ (n) the state of being able to live *freely*
housewife /ˈhaʊswaɪf/ (n) a married woman who works at home; she looks after the house and her family

behind his desk, waiting. Odette thought of her family and her home. Her heart ached as she spoke. "I'll help in any way I can. What do I need to do?"

Odette began her lonely life of secrets and lies immediately. She lied to her family. She wanted to be a war nurse, she told them. She smiled kindly as she kissed her daughters and husband goodbye. But, inside, her heart was breaking. "Will I ever see you again?" she thought.

The Secret Service gave Odette new French clothes, a French hairstyle, even a new French wedding ring. Odette's comfortable British life ended and her dangerous life as a spy began.

In November 1942 Odette started her work in Cannes, in the south of France. She looked and spoke like an ordinary Frenchwoman. But really she was working closely with a British spy, Peter Churchill, passing money to the French Resistance.*

Odette learned quickly. She started more and more dangerous work. She found "safe houses" for other spies to hide in. She also found new, secret places where British airplanes could drop guns and equipment. If spies are caught during a war, they are almost always killed immediately. Every word, every look, every thought was dangerous for Odette.

On April 16, 1943, Odette and Peter were caught by German police and questioned about their work. "This is the end," thought Odette. "The Germans will kill us." But then she had an idea. It was a dangerous plan, but it was their only hope.

"Don't kill Peter, kill me!" she said. "Peter is my husband. He doesn't work for the Resistance—he's only here for me." Did the Germans believe her? Odette thought quickly. She needed a better lie—a lie to save their lives. "Peter's uncle is the most important man in Britain! You'll die if you kill him!"

The Germans looked carefully at their reports. Who was this unusual woman? And who was Peter Churchill? *Churchill!* They could not kill this man. His uncle was *Winston* Churchill—the head of the British government.

* French Resistance: an organized group of French people who fought against the German government in France

"Take them away!" the German officer ordered. "Get every piece of information from them. Do everything that is necessary!"

When burning metal first touched her skin, Odette cried inside with pain. But her reply was always the same: "I have nothing to say." The cold, handsome man looked deeply into Odette's eyes. Then, slowly and calmly, he pulled out her **toenail**s. Odette did not make a sound. She was weak from pain, but she was proud. Her silence was saving lives across France.

A few days later Odette's future was decided. Her eyes moved around the courtroom slowly. It was a beautiful, clean room and the sun shone brightly through the large windows. She could hear the noise of busy Paris life outside.

But it seemed like a dream to her. Her feet were very painful and her body was weak, but Odette sat up straight and looked proudly into the officer's eyes.

"The court has decided that you must die," the German officer explained, in bad French. "You are a British spy and you work for the French Resistance. Return to your prison room and wait."

Days, weeks, and months passed. Each time the guards came to her prison room, death was possible. But Odette did not stop hoping. It seemed that her lie about Winston Churchill was working. Every night she imagined that she kissed her daughters. "I love you," she told them softly.

In May, 1944 Odette was moved to Ravensbrück, in the north of Germany. Here, hundreds of weak prisoners moved slowly between the long lines of simple buildings. Their bodies were thin, their heads were shaven, and there was complete hopelessness in their eyes. At Ravensbrück the prisoners worked until

toenail /'touneɪl/ (n) the hard, flat part at the end of a toe

they died. Every morning the dead bodies were burned, and the work continued. But someone had different plans for Odette in this terrible place.

Fritz Süren, the boss of Ravensbrück, was a cold, selfish man. He knew about Odette. He knew that she was special. But he did not **trust** her. He kept Odette alone and in complete darkness for months. But Odette knew how to stay hopeful. She imagined her family again, and in her mind she chose beautiful, colorful cloth and made pretty dresses for each of her daughters.

By now the Americans were in Germany and the war was almost at an end. On April 28, 1945, Süren visited Odette. "We are leaving today," he told her. He pushed her into a van with a few other prisoners. Through the window Odette could see German guards running, and cars and vans driving away quickly. She could not believe her eyes! "Will I live to go free?" she thought.

After four days of driving, a guard opened the van doors. He pulled Odette from the van and pushed her into Süren's car. "Why does he only want *me*?" she asked herself. She kept quiet and watched the road racing past outside.

Odette knew that Süren wanted to kill her. But hundreds of people were still alive because of her silence. She prepared for a proud death.

At 10:00 P.M. that night Süren drove Odette to a small town. "I'm giving you to the Americans," he explained. Odette could not believe her ears. Was this a joke? But Süren's face was serious. He thought that Odette was an important person. He wanted her to speak kindly of him after the war.

"This is Mrs. Churchill," Süren explained to an American officer. "She is a relative of Winston Churchill." Without looking at Odette, he dropped his gun. Then he turned slowly, and was taken by some soldiers toward his prison room. Odette looked around at the little town, the friendly faces of the American soldiers, and Süren's empty car by the side of the road. Was this a dream? Was she really alive? Was she really free?

Back in England, Odette fell into her husband's arms and cried happily. After years of fear and pain, her family was together again. Her daughters kissed and held their brave mother. "You look more beautiful than ever," she told them. "Your love gave me hope and kept me alive."

In 1946 Odette received one of the most important British medals for her great courage. "This is not for me," she said. "It's for all the French Resistance workers in the war."

Odette's brave actions saved thousands of French and British people. She loved her family, but she chose a dangerous and lonely life and helped others. Our lives today are shaped by women like Odette. We learn more about our present and our future when we remember their past courage.

trust /trʌst/ (n/v) a feeling that someone is honest and fair

Activities 4

4.1 **Were you right?**

Look back at Activity 3.4. Then answer these questions.

1   Why was the British government interested in Odette's vacation photos?

....

....

2   Where did Odette start her spy work?

....

3   Why did the Germans think that Peter Churchill was important?

....

....

4   How did Odette stay strong and brave in prison?

....

....

5   What did Odette get for her brave work?

....

....

4.2 **What more did you learn?**

Who are these people from Story 3? Read the sentences and write the correct name. Then write the correct sentence number, 1, 2, or 3, in the box on each picture.

1   .... was the head of the British government.

2   .... worked closely with Odette as a British spy.

3   .... received a medal for her courage.

4.3 **Language in use**

Look at the sentence in the box. Then choose one of the words from the box below to complete each of the sentences, 1–7.

> They fought hard **for** France's freedom.

against	at	by	in	into	to

1 Britain fought ....against............. Germany in World War II.
2 The Secret Service was interested .... Odette's photos.
3 As a spy, Odette had to lie .... her family.
4 Odette and Peter were caught .... German police in 1943.
5 By April 1945, the war was almost .... an end.
6 When she saw her husband, Odette fell .... his arms.

4.4 **What's next?**

Look at this picture of the Amazon rain forest. What do you know about it? Why is it important? Make a list in the box below.

Notes

Fighting for the Forest

Like forest people for thousands of years before him, Chico understood that man must use the rain forest carefully and thoughtfully.

The Amazon **rain forest** is one of the most wonderful places on Earth—the biggest, oldest, and richest forest in the world. It covers an area that is almost as big as Australia. It is home to millions of different kinds of animals, plants, and birds. Most of the world's fresh water is here, and the forest plants clean the Earth's air every day. It is very hot, wet, and dark. For man's future, the rain forest is probably the most important area in the world.

Chico Mendez was born near the Amazon town of Xapuri, Brazil, in 1944. There were no schools in the rain forest, and Chico started working at the age of nine. Like the rest of his family, the young boy earned money by taking small amounts of rubber from the forest's trees. The rubber was then sold to local factories. This is an old style of farming. The trees are not hurt when you take rubber from them. In this way, the forest and its people lived together comfortably.

As a young boy, Chico did not think about the world outside of his town, his family, and his work. But as he grew, he learned more and more about the rain forest. He learned how to use forest plants as medicines and for food. Like forest people for thousands of years before him, he understood that man must use the rain forest carefully and thoughtfully.

But people are often too selfish to think about the future. While Chico grew up, large areas of the rain forest were destroyed by greedy businesses. Near Xapuri, thousands of trees were burned to make new fields for modern farms. But without the forest, the land soon became dry and poor. Food and grass for the animals stopped growing in the new fields after only a few years. So the farmers cleared more trees for fields, and the problem became more serious.

rain forest /ˈreɪn fɔrɪst, fɑrɪst/ (n) a large area of tall trees in a warm area where there is a lot of rain

In other parts of the Amazon, the forest was burned to build roads and electricity stations. Many businesses cut down thousands of trees and sold the wood cheaply for furniture and paper. The rain forest is more than 180 million years old. When it is cut down, it will not simply grow back. It is gone for ever.

Chico felt very angry toward the businessmen and farmers near Xapuri. The rain forest was important and he wanted to save it. But Chico was just a poor rubber farmer. When he spoke to the businessmen, they did not listen. Money was too important to them. So Chico spoke to local politicians. But they were only interested in power. Chico was not important. He wanted people to listen, so he had to think of another way.

Chico started talking to ordinary people about the rain forest. He discovered that hundreds of people agreed with his ideas. His hope grew. "Many voices are more powerful than one," he thought. But the rich businessmen still did not listen. These powerful people, and greedy politicians, did everything possible to stop Chico's fight. Chico made many enemies in Xapuri at this time, and his life became more dangerous. But, like great men before him, Chico wanted to fight **peace**fully—with words, not with guns or knives. He knew that he had to change people's ideas.

Chico spoke to more and more people in the Xapuri area. He asked them about their work, and about the farms and businesses in their towns. Soon Chico knew about business and farming plans before they happened. So when big farmers or businessmen wanted to clear a new area of forest, Chico organized group meetings on that land. Soon hundreds of people came together in this way and stopped the work of the forest clearers. Large areas of the forest were saved.

But Chico's work meant that poor people—factory workers, truck drivers, and farm workers—were losing their jobs. Chico knew that he needed to find new jobs for these people. They needed jobs that did not destroy the rain forest. Then he had an idea that worked: People must stop cutting or burning the forest, but they could take forest fruit, plants for medicines, and rubber. People will look after the forest if they earn money from it. And they need a *healthy* forest to earn money now and for the future.

peace /pis/ (n) a time when there is no war or fighting

In the 1980s these were dangerous ideas. Business was very important to the Brazilian government. Brazil was not a rich country, but it wanted to help its people. Big companies brought in new money for better roads, houses, schools, and hospitals. So the government gave money to new farms. It paid people to burn the forest and to start new businesses. Most people agreed that this was good for Brazil. Chico was the first Brazilian man to speak out against new businesses. His ideas were very new and very strange.

It was almost impossible to change people's ideas. But, in Xapuri, parts of the forest were saved. This gave Chico hope. He knew that more people needed to understand his message. He also understood that money was very important. So he traveled around the country and explained the problem in a new way. When the forest is destroyed, two things happen: First, there is new land for new business or farming. This makes money quickly for Brazil and it is a good thing. But second, thousands of animals, plants, and trees are destroyed. Over time, these will give Brazil *more* money than factories or farms. Not everyone believed Chico's words. But scientists agreed that they were true. At last, people could begin to see a better future for the forest and for Brazil.

In 1985 Chico started a national group of forest workers. People across Brazil now knew about Chico's ideas, and most big Brazilian businesses knew about Chico's success in Xapuri. They started to worry. As Chico became more popular, he also made more and more dangerous enemies. Powerful politicians and businessmen were very angry about his work. Businessmen gave politicians large amounts of money and asked for help, and the politicians used their power against Chico. They made his life and work as difficult as possible. They even sent him to prison. But Chico did not stop fighting for the forest. He knew that his life was in danger. Many people wanted to see Chico dead. But Chico did not listen; he had other plans.

International companies owned many of the biggest farms and factories in the Amazon rain forest. Maybe personal conversations with the companies' presidents were the best way to save the rain forest for the world's future. It was difficult work for one man. But Chico knew that he was the best man for the job.

Later in 1985 Chico traveled to the United States and talked to many international companies. Some of the companies listened, and people around the US soon became very interested in this brave man from Brazil. The 1980s were big years for business and money in all of the world's richer countries. International business got stronger and many rich people became richer. But by 1985 there were people who wanted to believe in something more important. They wanted a safe and comfortable world for their children. Chico Mendez's intelligent message was not only about money; it was about the world's future. It was the message that people needed to hear.

In the next few years Chico's name became famous across the US and around the world. Newspaper reporters interviewed him, television producers made programs about him, and famous people wanted to meet him. More and more people sent money to protect areas of the forest. But across most of the Amazon area, big farmers and businessmen were still clearing the rain forests to make quick, easy money.

At last, some Brazilian politicians understood that Chico's ideas were important, too. The government started making plans to protect large areas of the Amazon rain forest.

In November 1988 Chico's ideas became part of Brazilian law. In some areas, people had to stop clearing the forest. But they could collect fruit, medicinal plants, and rubber in these areas. Chico worked hard to make more and more of these special areas. But as his dreams started coming true, someone stopped him in the only possible way.

Chico Mendez, the famous forest fighter, was murdered outside his home on December 22, 1988. Many people believed that they knew the killer—an important man in Brazilian government and business. But that was difficult to prove.

Chico's life was cut short, but his brave new ideas continued in other people. After his death, people around the world sent money to help Chico's work. More of the rain forest was protected, and big business lost some of its power. But people did not stop clearing the forest completely.

Today, man is still destroying thousands of square kilometers of the Amazon rain forest every year; hundreds of different animals and plants are lost every day. More than 20% of the forest is already lost for ever. It took millions of years to grow, but at this speed it will disappear completely in only fifty years.

We must not forget the work of Chico and people like him. One man changed the world's ideas. We have to think carefully about the things that we buy today. Our actions can save the rain forest. Chico's brave fight must continue.

5.1 Were you right?

Look back at your notes in Activity 4.4. Then finish these sentences.

1 The Amazon rain forest is probably the most important area in the world for man's f.*uture*................................ .

2 Big business was important to the Brazilian g................................ .

3 As Chico's ideas became more popular, he made more e................................ .

4 In 1988, some of Chico's ideas became part of Brazilian l................................ .

5 Many people believed that they knew Chico's murderer. But it was impossible to p................................ it.

5.2 What more did you learn?

Not all of people's actions are bad for the rain forest. Complete the box below with information from Chico's story. Add your own ideas.

Bad for the rain forest	Not bad for the rain forest
Burning trees for new farm land	

5.3 Language in use

Look at the sentence in the box. Then look at the pictures. What happened? Put the words in the correct order to finish the sentences.

The rubber **was** then **sold** to local factories.

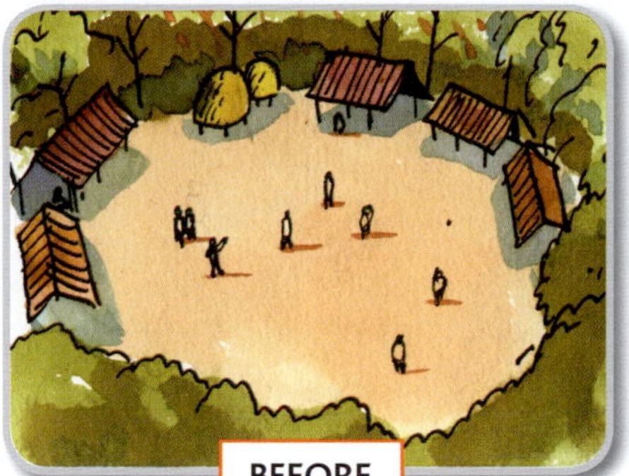
BEFORE

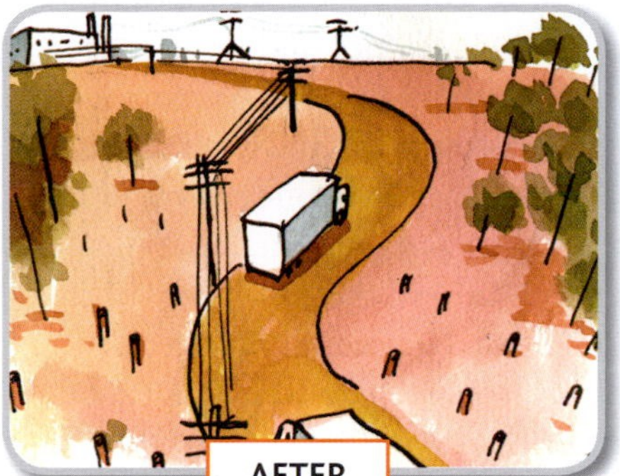
AFTER

1 Trees more cleared land to were make.

Trees were cleared to make more land ....

2 A built the road forest was through.

A ....

3 An was on the station land electricity built.

An ....

4 Many killed birds forest were animals and.

Many ....

5 People homes out moved were their of.

People ....

5.4 What's next?

Look at the beginning of Story 5 and the pictures on pages 26 and 27. Discuss these questions. What do you think?

1 What is a "Prisoner for Peace"?

....

2 What do you know about Aung San Suu Kyi?

....

Prisoner for Peace

Every day was a lonely, dangerous fight for freedom.
Suu could not move freely even in her own home.

Aung San Suu Kyi was born in 1945 to a rich and important family in Burma (now Myanmar). Her father was killed when she was only two years old. But her young life was happy and comfortable. When she was fifteen, the family moved to India. Suu became very interested in her mother's political work there. She understood the power of **politics** from an early age.

While studying in Oxford, Suu met Michael Aris, a handsome, young Englishman. Michael soon fell in love with Suu's Asian good looks and her bright intelligence. They married, and then traveled and worked in Asia for a few years together. Finally, they returned to England to live a simple, happy life with their two sons. But Suu could not forget her history, her family, and her people in Burma. She understood now that her father was killed during his fight for Burma's freedom. During the 1970s and 1980s, too, there were many problems in Burmese politics. As she read the newspapers, Suu remembered her father's courage.

In 1988 Suu visited her sick mother in Burma. It was a very difficult time for the country because the army wanted to form a new government. Many people were afraid of the future. Thousands of people, young and old, came into the streets to make their opinions known. But the army wanted power—they did not want to listen. They were ready to fight. Later that year, the army killed thousands of ordinary people. Suu knew that she had to choose between her comfortable, happy life with her family in Oxford and a difficult and dangerous life in Burma. Her mother was dying. Suu decided that she must continue her father's good work.

politics /ˈpɒlətɪks/ (n) the activities of *politicians* or other people who are interested in the government of a country

26

Suu understood a lot about international history and politics. She wanted to use the ideas of people like Martin Luther King and Mahatma Gandhi. In the United States and in India, these two men fought peacefully for the freedom of their people. She knew that the Burmese people wanted to choose their own government. They did not want the army to choose for them. She traveled around the country, and thousands of people listened to her speeches. The army watched Suu closely. She knew that her life was always in danger. But she believed that her country's freedom was more important. Suu was ready to fight—with intelligent words and ideas, not with guns.

In September 1988 the army took power. Suu and other politicians immediately started planning a way to return the government to the people. Then one morning early in 1989, a large group of soldiers came to Suu's home. "You must go back to England and stop your work in Burma," they told her. But Suu refused to leave. "If you don't go, you can't leave this house," they continued. "You are now a prisoner in your own home."

Suu continued to organize her political group from her prison home. The army watched her almost every minute of the day, but she carefully wrote secret letters and made secret phone calls. Every day was a lonely, dangerous fight for freedom. She could not move freely even in her own home, and her family could not visit her. But the terrible loneliness made Suu stronger and braver.

In 1990 the people of Myanmar voted for their country's government. Suu's political group, the NLD, won 82% of the votes. But the army refused to listen. They kept Suu in her home as a prisoner. And they refused to give power to the NLD. Myanmar's hopes for a better future were destroyed.

But Suu continued to work for her country. Her call for peace and understanding became famous around the world. In 1991 she won the Nobel Prize for Peace. Her two proud sons traveled to Norway and received the prize for her. She did not see them until a year later, when she was finally given permission for visits from her family. But her life as a prisoner continued.

Prison life made Suu stronger, the army thought. So they decided to let her go. In 1995 Suu finally left her house. She traveled around the country, calling for change. The army watched her very closely. Every new speech and every new trip was dangerous. But Suu did not lose her courage.

Early in 1999 Suu's husband became very sick. "Go and see him in England," the army suggested. But Suu did not trust them. "If I go home," she thought, "the government will tell me not to return." She knew that her husband loved her. She knew that he understood. When he died in March that year, her heart broke.

Television, radio, and newspapers in Myanmar are not free—reporters must always agree with the army's ideas. But Suu's speeches were full of different opinions. The army was nervous, and they asked her to stop traveling. She refused. In 2000 Suu became a prisoner of the army again. After her husband's death, she felt even lonelier than before. But she kept busy with political work, study, exercise, and piano playing.

For more than fifteen years, most of them as a prisoner, Suu has not stopped fighting. In 2002 she was freed again, but in 2003 the army attacked the NLD and many people were killed. Is the army beginning to listen more closely to Suu's ideas? Some people think so. After many years, Suu's courage still gives hope to her country's people—a hope for a future of peace and freedom.

A Mountain Accident

Aron pulled his arm, carefully at first,
and then more strongly, but it did not come free.

It was a beautiful spring day and 27-year-old Aron Ralston was walking in the mountains after a hard week at work. The air was fresh, and the sun was high in the sky. Aron stopped walking to listen to the silence of the mountains. "This is wonderful," he thought. "No work or noise. Only beautiful country around me."

As he continued on his way, he heard a low noise. He looked up quickly at the mountainside above him—but he was too late. Large pieces of rock were falling toward him and he could not escape quickly enough. The earth was moving, and the noise was terrible. In seconds, Aron's arm was caught under a rock that weighed 500 kilos.

The pain was terrible, but Aron stayed calm. He knew a lot about the mountains. He knew how to live in the wildest and most dangerous open spaces. He pulled his arm, carefully at first, and then more strongly, but it did not come free. Next, he pushed the rock as hard as possible. Again—nothing. It was getting dark. Aron ate a small amount of food and drank some of his water. He wanted to keep strong, get some rest, and try again in the morning.

After a difficult night's sleep, Aron thought carefully about his problem. Today was Sunday, a popular day for walking. He decided to wait for help to arrive. He looked hopefully up and down the narrow mountain path, but the mountains were empty and silent. The morning passed and the sun moved to the west. By late afternoon it was too late for walkers. Aron needed a different plan.

Using his climbing equipment, he tried to move the rock. He tried a number of different ways, but it was too heavy. Next, he took his pocket knife and tried to break away small pieces of the rock near his arm. "This will destroy my good knife," he thought, "but my life is more important!" But the knife failed to cut even the smallest piece of rock. Aron knew that he was really caught. He made himself as comfortable as possible for another lonely night.

Aron had enough water and food with him for a day's walk. But it was day three now and the food was almost finished. He only had enough for one more small meal. In his mind, a difficult and dangerous plan was growing, but he did not want to try yet.

It was Tuesday morning. After three difficult nights in the mountains, Aron was tired and hungry. He drank the last of his water and thought carefully. Now he knew that he had to cut off his arm. He took his knife from his pocket and bravely put the metal against his skin. He pressed down hard and began to cut. But after his work on the rock, the knife was not sharp. "I couldn't even cut the hair off my arm," he explained to newspaper reporters later.

Aron used the rock to make his knife sharp again. Then he cut through his skin as far as the **bone**. "Then I found that I couldn't cut the bone," he calmly told the reporters. For two more days Aron tried different ways to cut his arm off. Without food or drink, his body was getting weaker. But his mind was clear and strong. "I did what I had to do," he explained.

Aron turned his arm the opposite way to his body. The first arm bone broke easily. Then he broke the second. He tied a piece of cloth tightly around the top of his right arm to stop the blood. Then, slowly, he cut through the rest of his arm.

At last Aron was free! He looked down at his lifeless arm under the rock. It seemed like a strange dream. His clothes were covered

bone /bəʊn/ (n) one of the hard, white parts inside your body

in blood and the pain in his right shoulder was terrible. Aron felt very small and unimportant under the wide sky and tall, dark mountains.

Aron was still in great danger. He was a long way from home and he was losing blood fast. Darkness was only a few hours away. He had to get to a road as quickly as possible. He looked below him and thought carefully. It was an eighteen-meter drop to the valley floor, but it was the fastest way back. He had to try.

Aron started to lower himself down the steep mountainside. It was hard, slow work with only one arm, but finally his feet touched the valley floor. The nearest road was still sixteen kilometers away. There was no time to rest. Aron felt weak. It was difficult to think clearly. "I *am* going to do it," he told himself. "Just one step at a time ..."

Aron started walking. He had to reach help quickly. One more night in the wild mountains was too dangerous. Each painful step took him closer to help. But the walk was very long and difficult.

At last, after six hours, Aron saw two other walkers. He wanted to run and shout, but his body was too weak. When they finally saw him, the worried walkers gave Aron chocolate cookies and water. Then they moved him to open ground. Here, the flying mountain police found the group, and they took Aron immediately to the nearest hospital. For the first time, Aron knew that he was safe. He was truly alive!

Hours later, Aron lay quietly in his hospital bed and looked up at the shiny white walls around him. He was in a different world now—a small, safe world of men and machines. But part of him belongs forever to the wilder world of rock and mountain and sky. Aron says that he cannot wait to get out into the wild again.

6.1 Were you right?

Look back at your answers to 5.4. Which of the ideas below do you think Aung San Suu Kyi agrees with (A)? What does she disagree with (D)?

1 [A] Her father's fight for Burma's freedom was important.
2 [ ] You have to use guns to win fights.
3 [ ] Her country's freedom is more important than her own.
4 [ ] Burma's people do not want an army government.
5 [ ] Newspapers, radio, and television must always agree with the government.
6 [ ] Her husband could not understand her work.

6.2 What more did you learn?

Look at these pictures. What happened before and after each? Write a sentence in each box to complete the story.

1 Aron was walking in the mountains.

2 ....

3 ....

4 ....

6.3 Language in use

**Look at the sentence in the box.
Then answer these questions
in the same way.**

> They returned to England **to live** a simple, happy life with their two sons.

1 Why did Suu go to Burma in 1988?

....................To visit her mother...

2 Why did the Burmese go out into the streets?

....

3 Why did Suu stay in Burma after her visit?

....

4 Why did Aron try to move the rock?

....

5 Why did he tie cloth around the top of his arm?

....

6 Why did the other walkers take Aron to open ground?

....

6.4 What's next?

**Look at the beginning of Story 7. Who is Erin Brockovich? Have you seen
the movie with the same name? Circle words in the box below that will be
important in the story. What do you think?**

blood	drugstore
health	(information)
lawyer lie	money
passport	poison
prisoner	religion
secret	telephone
thief vacation	war
water	

The True Courage of Erin Brockovich

Erin was worried. Did PG&E want to hide something?
Were the people of Hinkley safe?

E*rin Brockovich* is one of Julia Roberts's best movies. It follows the life of a smart, young American woman with no husband and three young children. The movie has everything that a successful story needs: lots of action, strong people, and a happy ending. But most surprising of all, Erin's story is true.

Erin was in trouble. She had no money, no job, no husband, and three young children. Life is difficult when you are a single mother. But Erin loved her young family, and she wanted to make their lives happy and comfortable. Day after day she read the local newspapers and called for jobs. But every phone call and every interview was unsuccessful. It was time to try something new.

Erin visited her lawyer, Ed Massry. "I'm smart, I'm hardworking, and I'll do anything," she told him. "Please, give me a job!" It was a strange way to find a job. But Erin did what she had to do. She wanted to be a good person and a good mother.

Erin was not like the other office workers. She did not always speak politely, she did not wear dark suits, and she gave her opinions fearlessly. She worked hard, organizing papers into piles and boxes every day. But the work was too boring for a smart woman like Erin. Soon she started reading some of the letters and lawyers' papers to make her days more interesting.

Erin was a careful worker and she wanted to do her job well. One day she found some people's health papers in the same box as their house papers. This was unusual. "Why are these together?" she thought. "Maybe there's a mistake." She started looking at the big box of papers one page at a time. It seemed that a large electricity company, Pacific Gas and Electric Company (PG&E), wanted to buy hundreds of houses in the small town of Hinkley, close to their electricity station. But why? More importantly, why were the homeowners' health papers in the same boxes? It was a mystery.

Erin could not sleep that night. She was worried. Did PG&E want to hide something? Were the people of Hinkley safe? Erin was already a busy woman with her own problems. She had little time to worry about other people. But deep inside, Erin felt that something was wrong. Could she solve the mystery? She needed more information. The next day she spoke to her boss, Ed. With his help, Erin started looking more closely at the papers.

Erin discovered more and more strange papers in the Hinkley box. She realized that there was a serious problem. She loved her family and she wanted to spend more time with them. She wanted to see her children grow up. But people in Hinkley were very sick, and only Erin knew about it. She wanted to help. So she bravely decided to solve the Hinkley mystery alone.

Erin visited people in Hinkley and spoke to them about PG&E, their houses, and their health. She wanted to find the true story. Erin was not a lawyer. She was friendly and interesting and the people of Hinkley liked talking to her. They told her that PG&E was a good company. It made their water safe, it paid for their hospital tests, and it offered good jobs. But Erin was not so sure. Erin always got what she wanted. Now she needed help and information. She was working alone, but this did not stop her. She called and visited scientists, doctors, and lawyers. She talked to anyone who could help her. And every day she worked hard. At last, she got the piece of information that she really needed: PG&E was **poison**ing the water near Hinkley!

PG&E is one of the biggest companies in the US, and people liked and trusted it. But Erin realized that the company told lies. The water was safe, they said—but they were poisoning it. Erin was not important, famous, or rich. She was not even a lawyer. But she decided to fight against PG&E for the people of Hinkley. She knew that she had to help in every possible way.

How many people were poisoned in Hinkley? Was anyone in danger? Erin returned to the town to find out. People knew Erin now. They trusted her and they talked honestly about their health problems. Hundreds of people in Hinkley had terrible illnesses, and some were dying. As Erin listened to the great problems and worries in these people's lives, she became very angry. PG&E knew that it was killing people. It was expensive to clean the water from its electricity station. So the dirty water ran into Hinkley's river and drinking water. Now the company wanted to buy the houses and keep the secret. It was not worried about the people who became sick. It was worried about possible payments to those people.

Money was a big problem for Ed Massry, too at this time. Erin's work was important. He knew that. But lawyers only get paid when they win. It was

poison /ˈpɔɪzən/ (n/v) something that can make you very sick; if you drink a strong *poison*, you can die almost impossible for a small local law office to win against PG&E. Ed was afraid. But he was a brave man, too. He trusted Erin, and Erin's courage and hard work carried them through the most difficult times. From start to finish, Erin's work for the people of Hinkley took more than five years. During that long and difficult time, Erin and Ed made a great team.

As Erin talked to different Hinkley people, her name and face became famous in the town. She had to be careful, though—she did not want PG&E to know about her work. As more people told their stories, Erin got the necessary information. She worked longer and longer hours. She still had a family to look after, too. Her body and mind were tired. But she knew that quick action was important.

Finally, it was time to fight PG&E. Erin and Ed sent 634 notices for **lawsuit**s from their small office to the large, expensive offices of PG&E. It was brave—but was it crazy? PG&E was a dangerous enemy. Was this the end for Ed's company?

When PG&E received the notices for the lawsuits, its lawyers immediately realized the danger. The sick people of Hinkley wanted a lot of money from the company. More lawyers were brought in on both sides. The lawsuits were too big for Erin and Ed alone. But Erin continued to work on them. The Hinkley people were her friends now. She truly loved them, and she knew more about their lives and problems than anyone. So Erin, Ed, and the lawyers from other companies worked together to do their best for the people of Hinkley.

After months of hard work, important lawyers in expensive clothes filled a small courtroom. PG&E bosses sat quietly in their chairs, trying not to look worried. Erin was nervous and excited. She thought about her friends in Hinkley, and she remembered the long years behind her. As the judge spoke his final words, she listened silently.

PG&E had to pay $333 million to the people of Hinkley. It was the largest amount of money for this type of lawsuit in the history of the United States! This also gave hope to other ordinary people and small law offices. And when PG&E stopped poisoning the water at Hinkley, hundreds of people's lives were saved.

After their fight against PG&E, Erin and Ed had enough money to stop working forever. But today Erin is still working for Ed's office. She is not a lawyer—she always liked to do things her own way, and she has not changed. She says that she is proud of the movie. But her health, her family, and the people of Hinkley are more important. Today she works for other ordinary people who are fighting against big companies. Her courage and hard work continue to help people and save lives.

lawsuit /ˈlɔsut/ (n) a disagreement between two people or organizations that is taken to a court of law for a decision

A Doctor, a Father, and his Son

People can find courage at the worst times, Oe realized.
Deep inside, he had great strength, too.

Kenzaburo Oe, a writer, had a job to do. He was traveling to Hiroshima to write a story about its people for a magazine. But Oe's mind was not on his work. At home, in hospital, his baby boy was fighting for his life. His son was born seriously **disabled**. He was close to death. Oe loved his baby, but part of him almost wanted his son to die. Life with a disabled child is difficult. Oe was not sure that he was strong enough.

Oe stepped off the train into the warm August air. It was early morning and the city was quiet. Maybe it was a morning like this on August 6, 1945, he thought. On that day, American airplanes flew over Hiroshima and dropped the world's first **atomic bomb**. The world was never the same again.

Most people agree that this terrible bomb ended World War II. As a result, many thousands of lives were saved. But the bomb also destroyed thousands of lives in and around Hiroshima on that day. For years, people suffered and died from terrible, painful "A-bomb illnesses." Even today, sixty years later, people continue to suffer from the results of the A-bomb.

disabled /dɪsˈeɪbəld/ (adj) someone who cannot use a part of his or her body or mind in the usual way
atomic bomb (A-bomb) /əˌtɑmɪk ˈbɑm, ˈeɪ bɑm/ (n) a very powerful bomb; when it falls on an enemy city, it destroys a large area

As Oe thought about his son and the terrible history of Hiroshima, he felt sadder and lonelier. How could he ever find hope in this difficult world?

The next morning, Oe walked through Hiroshima's Peace Park toward the hospital. He wanted to interview the hospital's boss, Dr. Fumio Shigeto, for the magazine. As he pushed open the hospital doors, he immediately thought of his sick son. He wanted to escape from the clean smell of medicine quickly. But as Oe listened to the doctor's story, he became more and more interested in the problems of Hiroshima, and the courage of its people.

◆

On August 6, 1945, young Dr. Shigeto was waiting for a bus to take him to Hiroshima city center. Suddenly there was a bright light and a silent wave of heat. In seconds the A-bomb destroyed almost everything around it—buildings, trees, cars, and people. Luckily, the doctor was standing next to a strong wall, and he was not burned or killed. But seconds after the bomb, his ears were filled with the screams of people suffering around him. His position seemed helpless. But Dr. Shigeto calmly opened his black doctor's bag and began helping the person nearest to him.

The problem was much too big for one person, but nothing could stop the doctor. He worked bravely to stop the suffering. He did not rest for two weeks.

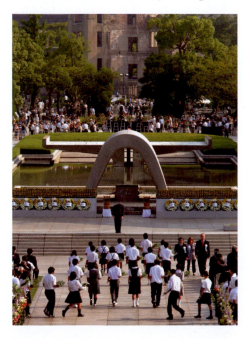

On the worst day in Japanese history, Dr. Shigeto did everything possible for the people around him.

◆

As Oe listened to Dr. Shigeto's story, he began to understand more about true courage. "Every day, a thousand people dead. But...I continued," the doctor explained. People can find courage at the worst times, Oe realized. Deep inside, *he* had great strength, too—enough strength to fight for his son's life.

Back in Tokyo, Oe visited his son's hospital and talked seriously to the doctors. "This was the most important change of my life," he said later. "I began to do something for my son, for myself, and for my wife."

For six years, Oe and his family worked hard to give their disabled child the best possible life. They played music to him and read him stories. "We love you," they told him. But little Hikari could not reply. At the most difficult times, Oe remembered Dr. Shigeto's courage. It always gave him the strength to continue.

Hikari loved the sound of birds singing, so Oe bought a cassette with bird songs and the birds' names on it. Hikari listened silently to the cassette for hours, still unable to speak. But Hikari wanted to tell his loving family, "I love you, too."

One day, Oe was walking in a small forest with Hikari on his shoulders. Suddenly, Oe heard a sound above him. He thought he was dreaming. "It's a water rail,"* the voice said. Oe stood in silence for five minutes, then it came again: first, the high sound of a bird singing, and then his son's clear voice, "It's a water rail."

Hikari could speak! After all their hard work, the Oe family could enjoy the results. Oe learned from Dr. Shigeto's courage. And now Hikari showed great courage, too. The young boy loved listening to music. It was difficult for him, but he learned to read music and play the piano. Slowly, with his family's help, he learned to speak, too. By the age of eighteen, Hikari was writing his own music—and people loved it. Today you can buy Hikari Oe's music in stores around the world. Music is his language, and the love of his family helped him as much as any medicine.

We cannot imagine the fear that Dr. Shigeto felt in Hiroshima in 1945. But millions of people around the world face personal difficulties like Kenzaburo and Hikari Oe's every day. Oe learned about courage from Dr. Shigeto. And Hikari learned to be brave from his father. In the same way, we can all learn about courage from the stories in this book. When times are difficult, remember these brave people. You, too, can find the strength and courage that you need.

* water rail: a type of bird. It lives near water.

1 Work in groups. Look at the pictures below and choose *key words* for each story. How are these three stories similar? How are they different? Finally, discuss the words you chose with the rest of the class.

War

Courage

Government

2 Who is the bravest person in this book, do you think?

a Discuss this question in small groups until you can agree on one person. Write the name and a list of reasons for choosing that person below.

b Discuss your decision with people in other groups. Do they agree? Why (not)?

Name:	
Reasons:	

Complete this court report about Erin Brockovich and PG&E. What information was given in court? What did the court decide?

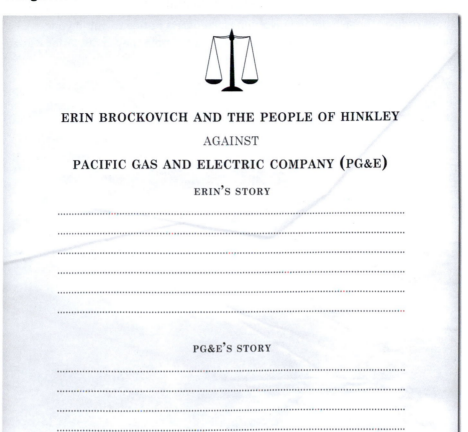

ERIN BROCKOVICH AND THE PEOPLE OF HINKLEY
AGAINST
PACIFIC GAS AND ELECTRIC COMPANY (PG&E)

ERIN'S STORY

....

....

....

....

....

....

PG&E'S STORY

....

....

....

....

....

COURT'S DECISION

....

....

....

....

....

....

WORK IN GROUPS OF THREE OR FOUR.

1 You work for *True Stories* magazine. The magazine wants to print some stories about ordinary people doing brave things. Prepare a notice to put in your magazine. Ask readers to send you stories about people they know. Offer a prize for the bravest person. Describe the prize.

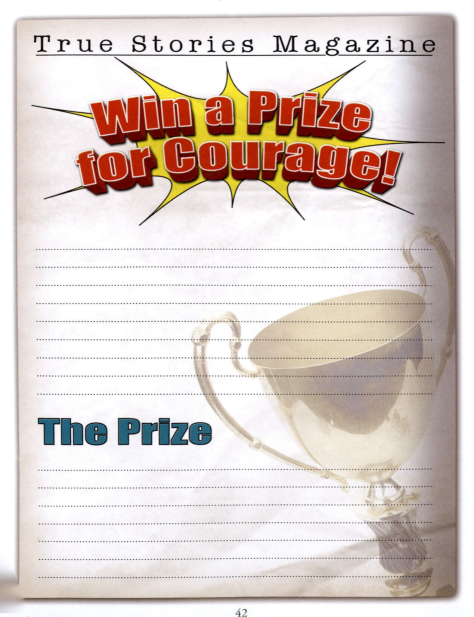

True Stories Magazine

Win a Prize for Courage!

The Prize

2 These people's photographs and stories were sent to *True Stories* magazine. In your groups, think of a name and imagine a story of courage for each person. Make notes below.

A

B

C

D

A

Name: .... Age: ....

Story: ....

....

B

Name: .... Age: ....

Story: ....

....

C

Name: .... Age: ....

Story: ....

....

D

Name: .... Age: ....

Story: ....

....

3 Imagine that each person in your group is one of the people above.

a Tell your story to the other people in your group and answer questions. Then vote for the best story.

b Listen to the best stories from other groups. Vote as a class for the bravest person.

4 Your magazine, *True Stories*, has chosen the winner of its "Prize for Courage." Write a story for your magazine about the prize winner, their story, and their prize. You can use one of the stories from questions 2 and 3, or you can write a new story.

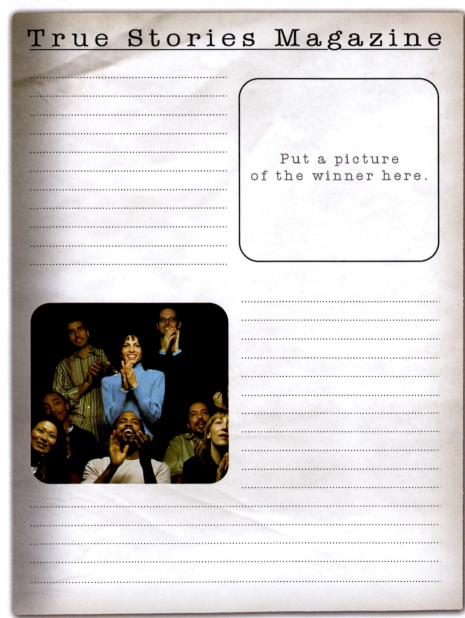

True Stories Magazine

Put a picture
of the winner here.